In this series –

THE ESSENTIAL

RUMI READINGS

THE ESSENTIAL
RUMI READINGS

Thirty-three extracts from
the *Rumi Readings* series, selected and
translated from the original Persian by
The Scheherazade Foundation

JALALUDDIN RUMI

The Scheherazade Foundation

The Scheherazade Foundation CIC
85 Great Portland Street
London
W1W 7LT
United Kingdom
www.SF.Charity
info@SF.Charity

First published by The Scheherazade Foundation CIC, 2025

THE ESSENTIAL RUMI READINGS

A CIP catalogue record for this title is available from the British Library.

ISBN 978-1-915311-85-6

Introduction

Jalaluddin Rumi was born in Balkh, Afghanistan, in the year 1207, and died in Konya, Turkey, in 1273.

During the sixty-six years spanning this pair of dates, he produced a range of extraordinary work in Persian which, today, is classed as 'Sufi Mysticism'.

In the seven and a half centuries since his death, Rumi's corpus, which includes *The Masnavi* and *Fihi Ma Fihi*, has been circulated widely across the Near East, the Arab world, and Central Asia.

Generations of students continue to commit selections of the 60,000 verses to heart, and allow Rumi's way of thought to permeate through all areas of their lives.

Although Orientalists venturing eastward from Europe in the 1700s occasionally made note of Sufi Mysticism, they tended to witness it through the more theatrical frills – such as 'whirling dervishes' – rather than through a deep appreciation of the texts.

It wasn't until the close of the nineteenth century that the first wholescale translations of Rumi's written work began to appear in Europe.

Even then, they remained very much the purview of a few academics, whose translations were – even for the time – laden with indescribably floral and cumbersome prose.

Although in the Occident, students would find themselves scrutinizing Rumi's corpus, it wasn't until more recently that accessible appreciations of his work became available.

A few years before his death, I asked my father – the Sufi scholar and thinker Idries Shah – for his thoughts on Rumi's legacy in the West.

Sitting in his favourite chair, a porcelain cup of green tea in hand, he looked at me hard.

'I never cease to be amazed,' he said.

'Amazed by what?'

'By the way people don't take what's perfectly packaged, and ready and waiting for them, but rather obsess with something else.'

'With what?'

'With endless and nonsensical trimmings, trappings, and paraphernalia.'

My father sipped his tea.

After a moment of silent thought, he continued:

'Read Rumi in the original Persian,' he said, 'and so delicate are the verses that you have tears rolling down your cheeks. Yet here in the West, it's served up as something submerged in a thick, glutinous gravy, so much so that its utterly inedible.'

I reminded my father that a series of publications had recently found their way to press – publications that presented Rumi's couplets in an utterly new way.

Stripped bare of what my father had referred to as 'gravy', they were light.

Indeed, they were lighter than light.

My father rolled his eyes at the thought.

'In any other place, and at any other time,' he said, 'people would be up in arms. Or, if they weren't, they'd be laughing until their sides split. Imagine it – Western poets with absolutely no knowledge of the original Persian text touting new, bestselling editions of Rumi's work! It's what we call "The Soup of the Soup of the Soup".'

In the years since my father's death, Occidental society has been flooded with all things Rumi.

Couplets ascribed to him are read solemnly at weddings across the United States, Europe, and beyond.

Wisdom drawn from his poetry is tattooed daily over the backs and limbs of Hollywood A-listers.

But the precious words uttered at weddings, tattooed into skin, and quoted in abundance, hold little or no bearing to the original verses of Jalaluddin Rumi.

So, there it is…

The great Sufi Master's wisdom available:

(a) in a form that's unreadable because it's all covered in glutinous gravy, or

(b) in another form that's completely distorted – the Soup of the Soup of the Soup.

One thing that *is* evident is that the West can benefit enormously from a clean, clear rendition of Rumi's thinking – as the East has done over the last seven hundred years.

For this reason, we have commissioned entirely new translations, gleaned in particular from *The Masnavi*. Selected and translated by native Persian-speaking scholars, the emphasis has been on maintaining the lightness of Rumi's poetry.

In an age of relentless speed and digital overload, and so as to allow the work to be accessed by those who may benefit from it most, we have arranged a series of bite-sized morsels by way of theme.

We encourage you to do what students, scholars, and ordinary people have done across the East for centuries...

To pick a single couplet, or a handful – and to read them over and over, allowing them to seed themselves in your mind.

Little by little, having taken root, they will blossom and bear fruit.

Tahir Shah

How to Use This Book

The Essential Rumi Readings is not a book to be read in a single sitting, nor one to be hurried through. It is not an anthology of poems for academic analysis, nor a manual to be followed step by step. Rather, it is a collection of living wisdom – carefully translated from the original Persian – designed to be absorbed, savoured, and slowly allowed to work its way into the fabric of your being.

This book invites you to pause, to breathe, and to open your heart.

It is a friend on the journey inward.

A Quiet Companion in a Noisy World

In an age of relentless speed, constant notifications, and digital overwhelm, the words of Jalaluddin Rumi arrive like water in a desert. They offer depth in place of noise, stillness in place of striving. But to receive their medicine, we must shift the pace at which we normally move.

Begin not with analysis, but with attention.

This book serves as an introduction to the wider *Rumi Readings* series in which wisdom from the Sufi master's work is presented in new compilations arranged around themes such as *Love, Grieving, Youth* and *Mental Health*. It is structured as a sequence of 33 selected reflections. Each one is drawn from Rumi's immense corpus, lovingly translated from the original Persian by scholars at The Scheherazade Foundation. Unlike many well-known English renderings of Rumi's work – often drawn from secondary or tertiary sources – these translations honour the spirit and the subtlety of the original voice.

The quotes are arranged in a flowing poetic arc: awakening, struggle, insight, love, letting go, and finally, transcendence. You may sense this rhythm as you move through the book – or you may find a different one altogether, shaped by your own inner landscape.

Either way, there is no single right way to read this book.

Read One Quote at a Time

One of the most powerful ways to use *The Essential Rumi Readings* is to read just one quote at a time. Let it be the first thing you see in the morning, or the last thing you sit with before sleep.

Don't rush past it. Read it slowly. Twice, or three times. Let it settle.

You may not 'understand' it at first – and that is perfectly fine. Rumi does not speak to the intellect alone. He speaks to the soul, the inner heart, the part of you that already knows, but may have forgotten.

Sit with the quote. Let it echo. You may find that what it means to you today is different from what it meant yesterday – or what it will mean years from now.

Let the Quote Find You

Sometimes, the best approach is not to search for the right quote – but to let the quote find you. Open the book at random. Trust that what you encounter is what you need.

In traditional Sufi practice, students have long consulted mystical texts in this way – letting divine coincidence guide the hand. You might be surprised by how often the right message appears at just the right time.

Let go of seeking. Let the words do their quiet work.

A Practice of Reflection

After reading a quote, try reflecting on it in silence. Ask yourself:

What is this speaking to in me right now?

What image or feeling does it stir?

Does it remind me of anything I've forgotten?

You may wish to journal your thoughts, to sketch, or simply to sit. There is no need to interpret the quote, nor to fully 'get' it. Often, its real work happens in the background of your awareness – like seeds planted deep beneath the soil.

Give it time. Water it with attention. Rumi's words are living – they grow.

Read Alone or Share With Others

You may choose to read this book entirely on your own, as a solitary practice. Or you may choose to share it with others – reading a quote aloud at the start of a gathering, in a meditation group, or around the dinner table with friends.

Rumi's voice has a way of opening hearts and softening spaces. Don't underestimate the power of reading a single line aloud, with sincerity.

These quotes have been used in therapy groups, grief circles, classrooms, and prayer spaces. They are not confined by doctrine or belief – they speak to the universal human longing for truth, for connection, for beauty.

Revisit, Reconsider, Return

This book is not linear. You may start at the beginning and move quote by quote, or you may jump around. You may read one quote every day, or return to the same one for weeks.

In fact, some of the deepest wisdom may lie in the quotes you feel resistant to – the ones that puzzle you, or that you don't like. Stay with them. They may be holding up a mirror to a part of yourself you've not yet seen.

Rumi wrote, '*In the embrace of pain resides mercy; freshness blossoms when barriers are broken. In times of darkness and cold winds, patience bursts forth in the heart of those who are broken. The elixir of life, the cup of ecstasy: these treasures lie hidden in the depths of adversity.*'

Let the broken place be your teacher. That is where patience flowers, where mercy stirs, where new life quietly begins.

Honouring the Source

These translations come from the original Persian, drawn especially from *The Masnavi*, which Rumi called 'the root of the root of the root of the faith'. They are not paraphrases, nor imaginative rewrites. They are careful, direct, and light-footed – an effort to bring the essence of the original text to life in the English language without distortion.

This matters. In a world where much of Rumi's work has been heavily reinterpreted – sometimes bearing little resemblance to the original – we offer these words as a return to source.

The Scheherazade Foundation believes that the true voice of Rumi, when heard clearly, needs no embellishment. It speaks for itself. It sings in silence.

Begin Again, and Again

There is no final 'completion' of this book. Like breath, it is something you return to again and again. What feels like an ending may lead you back to the beginning.

You will change. Your life will shift. And these same 33 reflections will meet you anew – each time, as though for the first time.

Let this be a space you revisit when you feel uncertain, when you're in need of beauty, or when words fall short. In Rumi's presence, silence is just as sacred as sound.

1

Make effort in this period
to free yourself from the limitations of time,
before the moment when time
ceases to have any meaning.

2

In the embrace of pain
resides mercy;
freshness blossoms when barriers are broken.
In times of darkness and cold winds,
patience bursts forth in the hearts
of those who are broken.
The elixir of life,
the cup of ecstasy:
these treasures lie hidden
in the depths of adversity.

3

Though you appear as a microcosm,
in your essence
you are the macrocosm.

4

The morsel serves as a seed
from which thoughts emerge;
the morsel symbolizes a vast sea,
and thoughts are its precious jewels.

5

The journey to the afterlife
is shrouded in mystery,
as it crosses a realm devoid of tangible landmarks.
Countless souls, linked like a chain,
depart continuously
through an imperceptible tear
in the fabric of the natural world.
Despite relentless searching,
this rift remains elusive,
yet it serves as the passage
to their ultimate destination.

6

The heart experiences peace
through honest expression,
as the thirsty find comfort in water.

7

Even the wise are destined to disappear,
serving as a lesson for those
who lack understanding.

8

Actions that originate
from your heart and soul
should be embraced and cherished,
just as you would cradle
your own child.

9

Because it draws you nearer to the friend,
thankfulness is the essence of blessings,
while blessings are merely their outer layer.

10

All things,
whether the moon or a fish,
offer praise with modesty,
but the teacher's wisdom
reveals it with greater clarity.
The stones shed tears,
and the heavens bestow blessings
when the teacher imparts lessons
of profound understanding.

11

Caution begets chaos; trust is preferable.
Rely on trust.
O ferocious one, do not wrestle with fate:
lest destiny wrestle with you in return.

12

Your transgressions have been
transformed by God,
turning all your past actions
into acts of compliance.

13

He made the world from grace,
and His sun shone on particles of matter.

14

Understanding deep emotion
is a valuable skill,
while grasping after superficial matters
is a heavy burden.
Profound knowledge
that resonates deeply within you
becomes a cherished asset,
while superficial knowledge
that only scratches the surface,
can be a hindrance.

15

Let go of your lower Self
and eliminate its flaws
through self-discipline
to achieve a state of contemplation.

16

With great care, bend the curve of the Self,
for it is evil and does not aid righteousness.
Even when it is given generously,
one could get a hundred times more in return.

17

Your dissatisfaction stems solely
from your longing for what you desire;
otherwise, all your desires
would be fulfilled effortlessly,
like gifts.

18

This teaching is intended for those
who choose to distance themselves from others,
and who lack awareness of the present moment.
Unless a person transcends sensory experience,
they will remain unaware
of the concealed, inner truth.

19

You are not merely an individual, dear friend;
you embody the universe
and a vast, deep ocean.

20

He asked,
'What wisdom lies in life and its mysteries
when the pure essence is confined in this shadowy realm?'
Clear water is hidden in the mud;
the pure soul is trapped within bodily form.

21

Embrace solitude
and choose seclusion
to prevent yourself
from being completely absorbed
by the world.

22

With each moment, an idea,
like a cherished visitor,
enters your heart anew.
Embrace each thought as it arises,
welcoming it with joy
and maximizing its potential.

23

O you who are the mirror of royal beauty,
O you who are the heavenly script,
everything that is in the world is within you.
Look within for what you seek,
because you are everything.

24

As I have died before my natural death,
I have conveyed this resonance from beyond.
Therefore, awaken to the Day of Judgement
and observe it;
perceiving anything necessitates this condition.

25

This silence is like a great ship
crossing the expansive ocean of Truth.
As a sea-worthy vessel
is needed for turbulent waters,
so silence is required for self-expression
in the depths of comprehension.

26

Those who reach unity
express it in stillness.
Their mouths remain silent
while their eyes, turned from the world,
reveal the beauty within.

27

Those who embark on the path without a guide
may turn a two-day trip
into a journey of a hundred years.
Anyone who rushes to the Kaaba
without proper guidance
will become disoriented and embarrassed,
and wander aimlessly.

28

The pursuit of desires is deceptive and fleeting,
like a dark illusion surrounding a brief glimmer of light.
This light of temptation and metaphor,
like a spark, dances in the shadows,
leading you down a long and winding path.
Your words and actions are ignored
and your journey remains uncharted.
You stumble, sometimes falling into the depths,
sometimes grazing the surface,
all the while unaware of your true destination.

29

Within us reside myriad wolves and swine,
both pure and evil,
virtuous and vile.
The dominant being governs all,
like the superiority of gold over copper
when both are shown side by side.

30

Rational thought, much like the angel Gabriel,
can offer guidance,
but if it leads you astray, it can cause harm.
As the sovereign of your soul,
you must recognize when to stop letting it direct you,
as its scope is limited.

31

Look within and abandon fruitless searching;
search inside yourself rather than
constantly seeking validation from others.

32

The pain of love
is the path to wholeness,
and the obstacles we encounter in love
outshine the tranquility
of the mundane world.

33

The paradox is this:
the beloved encompasses both unity
and your own existence.
Within the beloved lie both beginning and end.
Once found, all waiting dissolves,
for it is both revealed and concealed,
a hidden knowledge.

Finis